TREE HOUSES
BY ARCHITECTS

TREE HOUSES
BY ARCHITECTS

JAMES GRAYSON TRULOVE

HDi
HARPER
DESIGN
International

An Imprint of HarperCollins Publishers

Tree Houses by Architects

Copyright 2004 © by James Grayson Trulove and
Harper Design International

Published in 2004 by
Harper Design International, an imprint of
HarperCollins*Publishers*
10 East 53rd Street
New York, New York 10022-5299

Distributed throughout the world by:
HarperCollins International
10 East 53rd Street
New York, NY 10022
Fax: (212) 207-7654

HarperCollins books may be purchased for educational, business, or sales promotional use. For information,
please write: Special Markets Department, HarperCollins Publishers Inc., 10 East 53rd Street, New York, NY
10022.

Packaged by:
Grayson Publishing, LLC
James G. Trulove, publisher
1250 28th Street NW
Washington, DC 20007
202-337-1380
jtrulove@aol.com

Library of Congress Control Number: 2004101862

ISBN: 0-06-057286-8

Printed in China
First printing, 2004
1 2 3 4 5 6 7 8 9 / 06 05 04 03

Half title page: Tee Hee House, Richard Leo Johnson, Photographer
Title page and page 6: Tree Loft, Kenneth M. Wyner, Photographer

CONTENTS

FOREWORD

Tree houses come in all shapes, sizes, and configurations, from homemade backyard specials to elaborate dwellings suitable for full-time living. To think of a tree house is to bring back memories of childhood, of adventure, of the freedom of a bird perched high above the ground in a leafy hideaway.

In preparing this book, we decided to approach the subject from three points of view: classic tree houses, experimental tree houses, and houses in trees. Classic tree houses most closely approximate the fairy-tale notion of what a tree house should really be. Most are carefully nestled into the branches in such a way as to not damage the tree itself. Projects included in this volume range from a tree house for a science museum designed by the Texas architectural firm Lake/Flato, to a portfolio of classic tree houses designed and built by the TreeHouse Company, a firm based on the west coast of Scotland.

Experimental tree houses could not be more different. Here, designers attempt to push the envelope in terms of the design and materials used to construct the tree house. One such tree house, designed by Osamu Ishiyama in Japan, can accommodate wheelchairs; another, by architect Jeff Etelamki, uses industrial materials to construct a duplex tree house for two young children.

Houses in trees represent something of a hybrid since the primary objective is to celebrate and integrate existing trees on the building site into the overall design of the house, or to create a soaring, lofty space that at least creates the illusion of living high in the trees. In all cases, the site is a determining factor in the shape, size, and construction methods employed in the realization of the project. The Tree Loft by architect Travis Price is a striking example. Set on a steep hillside that was considered virtually unbuildable, it was made possible by erecting two massive steel columns that literally suspend the house above the ground, mimicking the trunks of real trees.

All of these projects share a common desire to thrust the occupant into the midst of the forest, defying gravity while offering a secluded sanctuary.

CONTEMPORARY TREE HOUSES

LOMAC TREE HOUSE

SAFDIE RABINES ARCHITECTS
UNDINE PROHL, PHOTOGRAPHER

This cedar, glass, and aluminum tree house is nestled within a grove of eucalyptus trees overlooking a lush canyon in San Diego. The 1400-square-foot house is perched on stilts, and an exterior staircase climbs to a spacious mahogany porch. A long, slender, aluminum and wood trellis leads to the front door. Inside, the house opens to its surroundings. The organization of the house is simple, with all vertical circulation to one side, eliminating hallways.

The interior and exterior living space is spread out over four half-levels. The large expanse of sliding glass pocket doors, which make up three sides of the living room, opens the home to its decks and terraces, reaching from the inside out into the trees. The house appears to float in between the branches, making the small house feel light and spacious.

Due to the condition of the site, the narrowest part of the house faces the canyon. To maximize views, the rooms on the east side of the house are higher than those facing the canyon on the west. The rooms themselves are deliberately kept open to allow sight lines to flow from one room to another and through the trees to the canyon.

Clerestory windows wrap around three walls of the dining room, bringing in light and views of the treetops, while the windows in the adjoining kitchen are positioned low, allowing for views of the gardens below. The kitchen, finished with dramatic surfaces of zebra wood cabinetry and stainless steel, has a centrally located black-slate topped kitchen island and a blue-and-gold macaw calling from her large custom-made cage.

◀ At home with the birds.

▶ The roof deck is perfect for entertaining amid the trees.

▶▶ The entrance is marked by a slender aluminum and wood trellis.

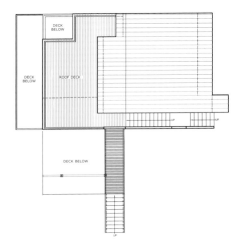

DECK
BELOW

DECK
BELOW   ROOF DECK

DECK BELOW

UP   UP

UP

0 1'2' 4'   8'

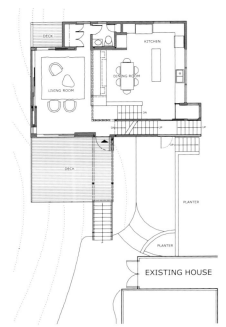

DECK

KITCHEN

LIVING ROOM

DINING ROOM

DN   UP

DECK

PLANTER

PLANTER

EXISTING HOUSE

DECK

BEDROOM

CL.

CL.

MASTER BEDROOM

DN

UP

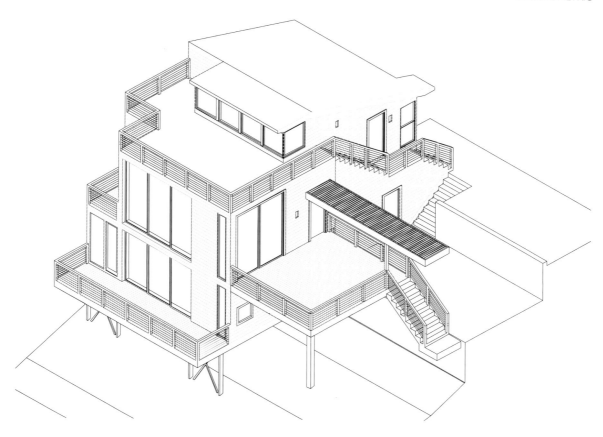

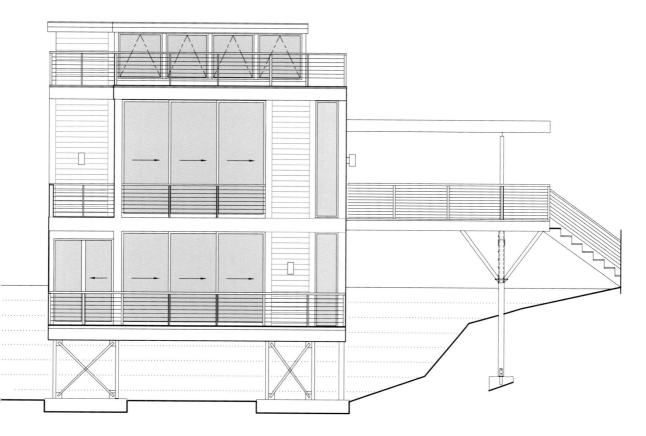

▲ Conceptual sketch.

▶ North façade.

▲ Sliding glass pocket doors make up
three sides of the living room.

▲ The dining area.

▶ The treetops are visible through the clerestory windows that wrap around the dining room.

▶▶ The entry.

◄ The master bathroom
shower opens onto a deck.
►► The high decks encourage
bird watching.

HEXENHAUS

ALISON & PETER SMITHSON, ARCHITECTS
ROLAND HALBE, PHOTOGRAPHER

The development of this project occurred over a 17-year period as a close collaboration between the client and the late architects Alison and Peter Smithson. Over the years, additions were made to the existing sandstone and timber house, all in the spirit of connecting the dwelling with its wooded, hilly site. It is known as the Hexenhaus (German for "witch's house") because of its location in an area made famous by the Grimm Brothers' fairy tales.

Surrounded by 400-year-old oak trees, two tree houses have been constructed. The first is a small lookout tower connected by a narrow bridge from the main house. The second is referred to by the owner as his holiday home and as the Hexenbesenraum—the witch's broom closet. Resting on nine oak poles over 40 feet in height, it has floor-to-ceiling windows, its roof is partially glazed, and its floor is made entirely of glass.

▲ View of the main house from the Hexenbesenraum.

▶ With its extensive glazing, the Hexenbesenraum glows warmly at night.

▶▶ Glazing is limited on the south and east sides.

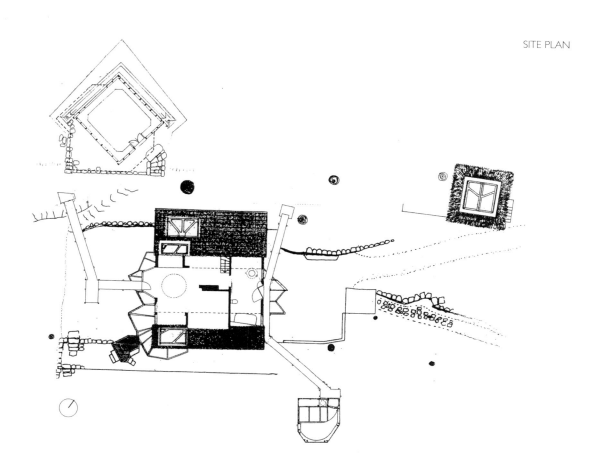

▲ View of the Hexenbesenraum from the
main house.

▶ Connecting bridge detail.

▶▶ View of the lookout tower from the
main house.

▲ ▶ The lattice bars on the
windows and doors of the
Hexenhaus mimic the branches
of trees.

▲ The master bathroom and
bedroom of Hexenhaus.
◄ The lattice bars frame surrounding views.

▲ Interior view of the
Hexenbesenraum showing the
glass floor.

▶ View of the main house at
night.

Soaring spaces and commanding river views distinguish this slender tower perched on a steep site above the Potomac River. Helical steel piers, some more than 60 feet long, provide stability for the structure, and a steel frame provides the necessary rigidity to the four stories of glass. Teak sunshades protect the steel and glass façade from the south sun. Inside, a wall of books extends up through three stories climbing parallel to the stairs.

COZZENS HOUSE

McINTURFF ARCHITECTS
JULIA HEINE, PHOTOGRAPHY

◀ Teak sunscreens on the river elevation.

▲ ▶ The double-height living room
with a view of the river and bridge.

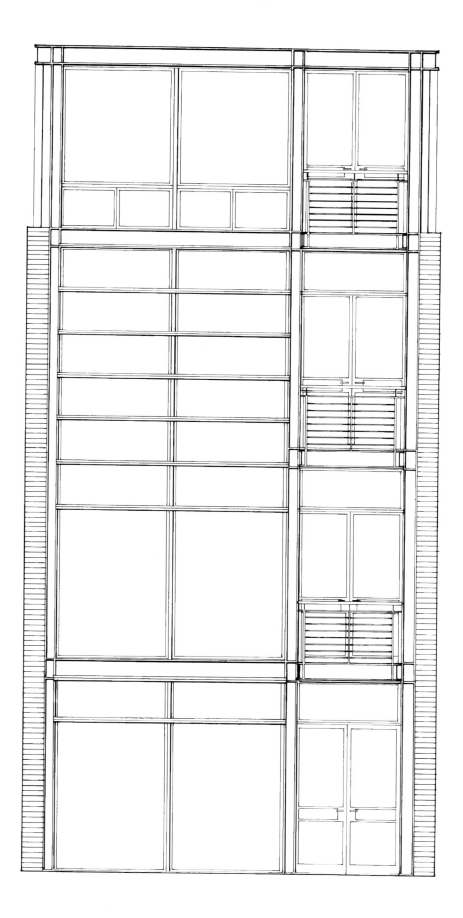

◀ Model

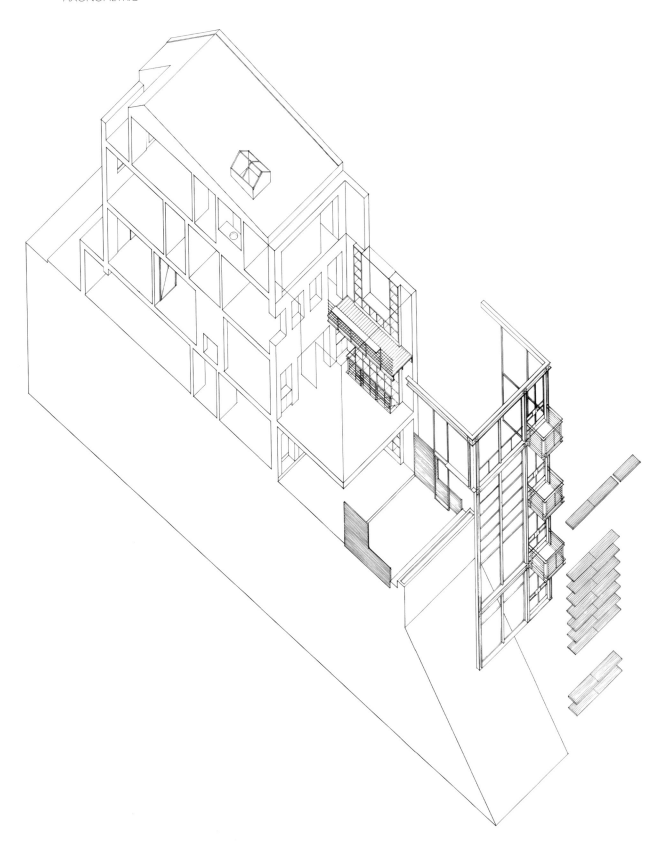

THIRD FLOOR

SECOND FLOOR

ENTRY LEVEL

LOWER LEVEL

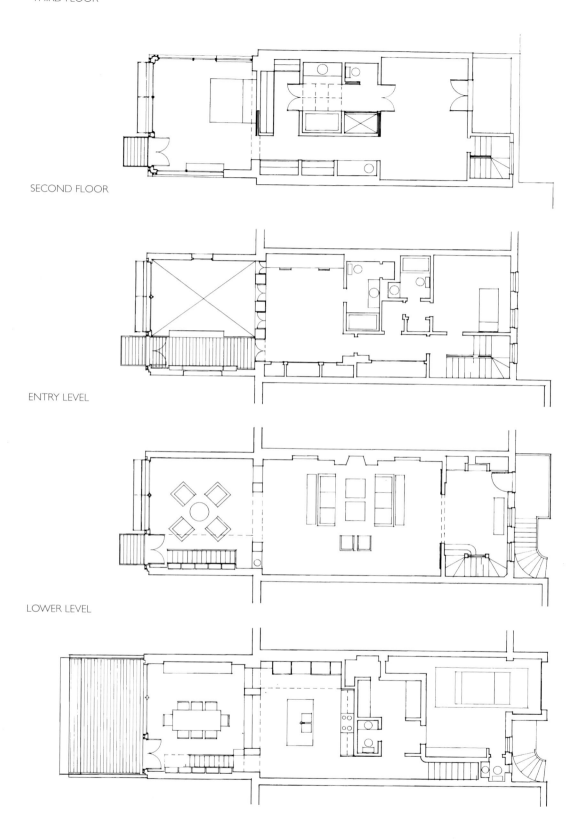

▶▶ View from master bedroom.

LEDGE HOUSE

BOHLIN CYWINSKI JACKSON
KARL BACKUS, PHOTOGRAPHER

Constructed of heavy white cedar logs, this is a house in the trees and of the trees. Placed at the edge of a small plateau on a forested mountainside, the house overlooks a stream valley. The shed roof is detailed with galvanized steel connectors and supported independently of the log walls. The natural look of the log timber post-and-beam construction on the exterior of the house gives the illusion that the structure is growing out of the forest. The interior uses select Douglas fir timbers, rafters, columns, and beams selected for aesthetic and structural qualities.

◀ The house is sited on a stone
ledge.

▼ Entrance

▲ The house is carefully integrated

into its natural surroundings.

▶ Detail of the galvanized steel

roof connectors.

▲ The rustic construction is
evident in every detail.
◄ A footbridge extends over
the stream.

◄ The living area

▶▶ Massive Douglas fir timbers and white cedar logs define the interior.

◄ An indoor pool extends along the stone ledge.

►► Perched on the ledge, the house enjoys a commanding view of the treetops.

TREETOP HOUSE

WHITNEY POWERS, ARCHITECT
EDWIN GARDNER, PHOTOGRAPHER

Stringent building restrictions on this ecologically protected island off the South Carolina coast mandated that no trees be destroyed when constructing a house on the island. This created a challenge for the architect since the only building site on this lot was populated with large oak trees. The architect's design solution was to build up and among the trees, placing the 4000-square-foot dwelling on wood pilings 12 feet above the ground. The large treetop family room has panoramic views of the surrounding landscape and the ocean. Eight screened porches enhance the sensation of living in a tree house, while a 75-foot bridge skips across the wetlands to a small pavilion near the ocean.

While protecting the natural surroundings, significant effort was made to employ principles of green design in the construction of the house, which relies heavily on natural light and ventilation. Handcrafted, double-hung cedar windows, numerous French doors, louvered doors in all the bedrooms, and ceiling fans allow a constant ocean breeze to flow through the house.

▲ Twelve-foot pilings lift the house into the trees.

▶ To enhance the treetop experience, porches are on every level.

▲ ▶ View of the bridge to the

beachside pavilion.

▶ ▶ View of the kitchen and living

area.

◄ View of the wetlands and beach from the top of the house.

▲ The bridge makes minimal contact with the land.

▶ View of the house from the pavilion.

TREE LOFT

TRAVIS PRICE ARCHITECTS
KENNETH M. WYNER, PHOTOGRAPHER

This structure resembles an abstract tree, its four floors wrapped in patina copper and glass and suspended high on a 100-foot cliff by two trunk-like 18-inch-in-diameter columns of steel. Set on 10-foot-deep concrete foundations, the 65-foot columns support the entire mass of the house. Two 5000-pound concrete-filled steel wells hang from the bottom level to counterbalance excessive wind loads. All of the runoff water from the house is recycled on site for irrigation, with the excess returned to the streambed below.

Every large tree on the site was preserved due to the minimal foundations. As a consequence, the house has been literally built around the trees. Entry is via a glass bridge through a small glass portal cut into a soaring space paneled entirely in wood. The 3,300 square feet of interior space accommodates three bedrooms and baths, living and dining areas, and a guest studio.

◀ A glass corner composed of super-insulated glass.

▶ View from the streambed.

◄ Front entrance with a cutaway in the

copper cladding to accommodate an

existing oak tree.

▲ Detail of the cutaway.

◀ ▲ ▶ Details of the structural system that suspends the house above the cliff.

◄ View of the cantilevered master bath shower
from above.

▲ View of the roof of the master bedroom and the
steel columns.

►► Exterior and interior views from the middle
level, where the galley kitchen is located.

◄ Two-story living room with Kalwall
transparent fiberglass panels.

▲ The spiral steel stair connects the four
levels of the house.

◄ Second floor hallway to the bedrooms.

▲ Entry to the master bath with a corner window in the shower.

▶ Shower detail with a cutaway window wrapping around an existing oak tree.

◄ Dusk view showing master bedroom tower and cantilevered master bath shower.

GIPSY TRAIL HOUSE

ARCHI-TECTONICS

PHOTOGRAPHS COURTESY ARCHI-TECTONICS

This lakefront residence is tucked into the hillside, its base constructed of rough stone collected on site. Cantilevered above the stone base is the main living area. Large steel beams support generous floating terraces among the trees. The core of the second floor contains the kitchen, bathrooms, fireplace, heating, and cooling systems. In the center of the roof, over one of the bathrooms, is a skylight made of glass planes. Where the roof meets the wall, in the shower stall, the glass planes continue and form the wall of the shower stall.

The ground floor has direct access to the lake via a recessed, hidden path, where an outdoor hot tub and shower are built into the rocks.

▲ View towards the living room.

▶ View of skylight wrapping over

the bathroom.

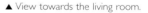

▲ View from property.

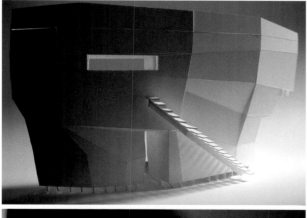

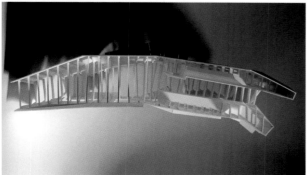

▲ Entry stairs to the main

level.

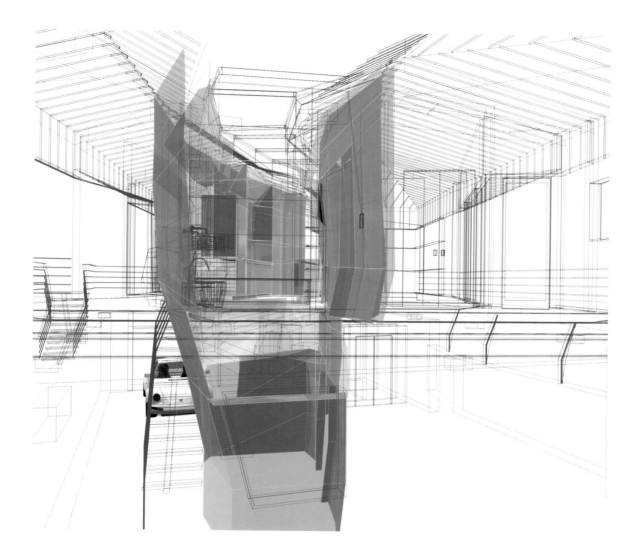

▲ Cedar cantilever detail.

◄ Steel beams support the large float-

ing terraces.

◄ View of terrace off of the living

room.

▲ Kitchen

◄ Foyer

◀ Glass planes form a
continuous skylight.
▼ View of skylight from the
interior.

CLASSIC TREE HOUSES

TEE HEE HOUSE

CANDACE LONG BREWER,
LANDSCAPE ARCHITECT
LISA TORBETT INTERIORS
RICHARD LEO JOHNSON, PHOTOGRAPHER

Nestled among centuries-old oak trees, this board-and-batten tree house boasts commanding views across marshlands to the river. It rests on 12-by-12-inch poles and was designed and constructed to conform to current building codes. The Tee Hee House's standing seam metal roof is evocative of surrounding houses in this "Low-Country" locale. It was professionally decorated and set among carefully landscaped grounds, providing a quiet escape for painting or reading.

▶ The landscape provides a complementary setting for the rustic tree house.

▼ Entry

▲ Entry

◄ The shark tooth fascia adds a whimsical touch.

▲ View over the landscaped
grounds.
▶ The house is constructed
among large oak trees.

▲ The interior was professionally
decorated.

SCIENCE TREE HOUSE

LAKE/FLATO ARCHITECTS
PAUL HESTER, PHOTOGRAPHER

This tree house has become the identifying element for the Witte Museum in San Antonio, Texas. The multi-level, open-air structure was constructed among the existing live trees, resting upon a stained ferro-cement rendition of two oak trees. There is an upper and lower tree house that recall the old W.P.A. concrete "trees" existing in the park. The Science Tree House is accessed via stairs and ramps that wind around and through real trees and connect back to the museum itself. The tree house overlooks the San Antonio River and is equipped with binoculars for observing local wildlife.

▶ Entry to the tree house.

◀ The stained ferro-concrete structure was created by sculptor Carlos Cortes.

▶ Model of the tree house.

▼ Sketch of the museum com-
plex that includes the tree
house.

◄ ▲ All "wooden" elements of the tree
house are made out of sculpted concrete.

▲ The San Antonio River flows

beneath the lower tree house.

◄ The entry to the tree house.

▲ A view of the tree house and

the museum building.

ACKERGIL TOWER

TREEHOUSE COMPANY
PHOTOGRAPHS COURTESY TREEHOUSE COMPANY
WWW.TREEHOUSE-COMPANY.COM

This tree house is one of the largest such projects in the United Kingdom and can accommodate conference space and dining for 30 guests. Its design incorporates two unusual self-seeded sycamore trees within a walled garden. A spiral staircase leads to the main entrance, which is flanked by two large tree trunks. A third trunk runs through the reception area and out through the roof.

▲ Roof detail

◄ The tree house is capped by a high tower peering through the branches.

▲ Dining area

▶ A large trunk runs through the

reception area and out the roof.

▲ The tree house is lit dramati-

cally at night.

◀ Two large tree trunks frame

the entrance.

CLASSICS
PORTFOLIO
PHOTOGRAPHS COURTESY TREEHOUSE COMPANY
WWW.TREEHOUSE-COMPANY.COM

Tree houses in this section were designed and built by the TreeHouse Company. Headquartered in Scotland, it has built over 500 tree houses in Europe, the Caribbean, Africa, and Russia. The projects shown in this portfolio section represent a broad range of designs and uses, from backyard offices, to children's tree houses, to fully functional dwellings.

◀ Considered the world's largest tree house, Alnwick Gardens Tree House appears as if suspended in this grove of mature lime trees.

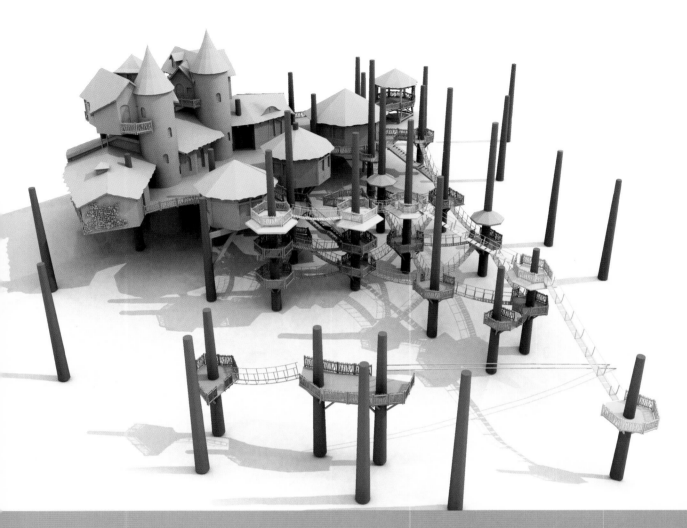

▲ Computer model.

▶ Roof and deck rainwater is collected into an underground tank and redistributed to the trees to compensate for the dry area around the trees caused by the large structure.

▲ A four-level children's

tree house.

▶ This tree house serves as

an office.

▲ Tucked in the branches of a
weeping willow tree, this
dwelling appears to be suspended over the river.

◀ This tree house is connected
via a rope bridge to a deck
used for entertaining.

◄ Constructed within a group of Scottish pines, this family compound consists of an upper level children's tree house with a lower level for the parents.

▲ ▶ This tree house was

designed to be an office.

◀ Nestled in a mature oak tree, this award-winning tree house features a thatched roof.

▲ This tree house is a swimming
pool changing room constructed
entirely in cedar with hand-carved
roof detailing.

◄ The dining room in this tree house
was designed to accommodate over
20 adults.

▲ ▶ This tree house is nestled in the
boughs of a great sycamore tree overlooking a tennis court.

EXPERIMENTAL TREE HOUSES

ACCESSIBLE TREE HOUSE

OSAMU ISHIYAMA LABORATORY
PHOTOGRAPHY COURTESY OF OSAMU ISHIYAMA LABORATORY

Creating a tree house for the physically disabled would seem to be a daunting task, but the Japanese architect Osamu Ishiyama has created a structure that is not only accessible but sculptural and poetic as well. "Imagine floating in the forest in a wheelchair," he writes, "listening to all of the sounds of nature and touching the texture of the trees, feeling their pulse, discovering the freedom of the trees rooted in the earth." The lightweight tree house is constructed of wire mesh mounted on slender steel poles. It is sited on a steep hillside and is accessible via wheelchair from the top of the hill. The porous wire mesh walls enhance the feeling of floating in space that the architect sought to achieve.

▲ The tree house cantilevers
out over the hillside.

▶ It is anchored on the hillside
and supported by steel poles.

▲ ▶ ▶▶ In the tree house, the
architect wanted to create a space in
which both one's body and mind
could experience a sensation similar
to that of floating in space.

SPHERICAL TREE HOUSE

TOM CHUD DESIGNER / BUILDING
PHOTOGRAPHY COURTESY OF TOM CHUD

This 9-foot in diameter sphere is constructed of yellow cedar strips covered with two layers of woven fiberglass roving set in epoxy. The sphere and the web of ropes that support it are attached to separate trees, distributing the load of approximately 500 pounds. The sphere is accessed by a spiral stairway and a short suspension bridge. Inside, the sphere is insulated and vinyl upholstery fabric is attached to the frames. It is wired for power, sound, and telephone.

► ▼ The sphere's weight is supported by several different ropes, so if one breaks the remaining ropes can carry the load.

◀ Stair detail

▼ Entry

▲ View of sphere from below.

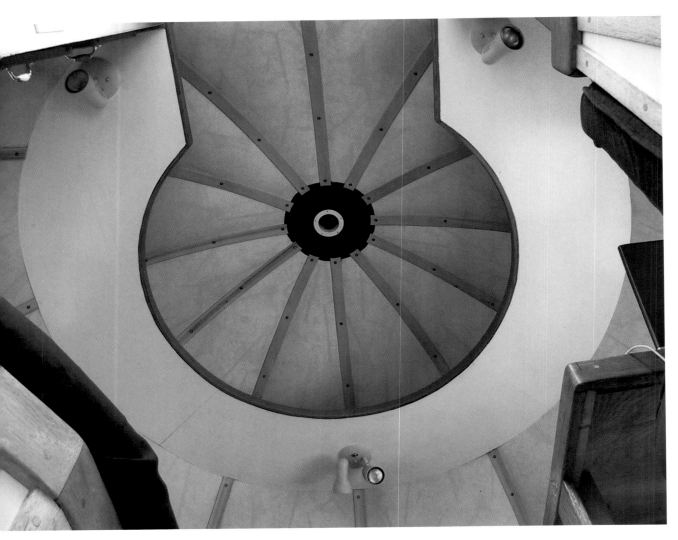

▲ A spiral stairway rises up

to the sphere.

◀ Interior views

FLOOR PLAN

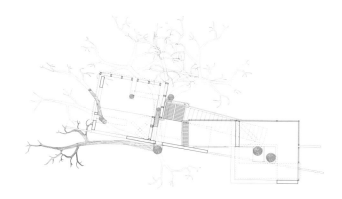

ROOF PLAN

ELEVATION

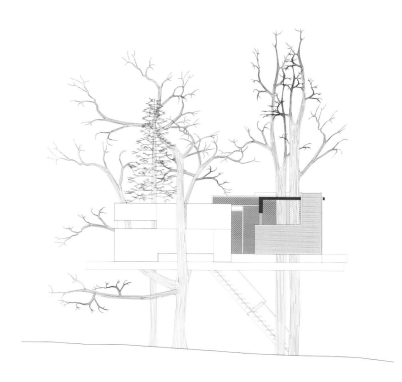

▲ Walls are constructed of safety-

orange fiberglass strips.

◀ The strips filter the light.

▲ A view of the two distinct houses from the ground.

▶ A view of the bridge.

◄ ▲ Openings allow branches
to penetrate the structure.

◄ ▲ Materials were chosen to

evoke the "found object" vernacular

of the tree house.

DUPLEX TREE HOUSE

JEFF ETELAMKI, ARCHITECT
PHOTOGRAPHS COURTESY JEFF ETELAMKI

This project was commissioned by a father with two young daughters for their weekend enjoyment. Each child was asked to prepare lists and drawings describing their playhouse needs. It soon became clear that each wanted her own tree house. Two adjacent trees were identified on the property, and the architect devised a scheme that resulted in two connected tree houses. The design seeks to create a unified structure with two distinct houses. They are connected by a Z-shaped bridge and support beams that allow for movement between the tree houses. Industrial materials were used in the construction of the 64-square-foot houses, including corrugated galvanized steel, chain link threaded with fiberglass strips, corrugated fiberglass, and rubber roofing.

▲ The duplex appears to be a unified structure.

◄ It is accessed via a formal staircase.

CONCEPTUAL SKETCH

STRUCTURAL SKETCH

STRUCTURAL SKETCH

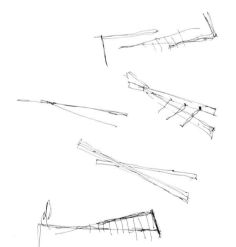

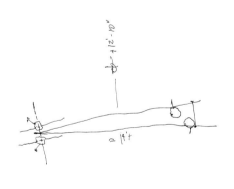